PANAYIOTIS KALORKOTI

An Exhibition

of

Acrylics, Watercolours & Etchings

17 December 1997- 7 March 1998

Design Works
William Street
Felling
Gateshead NE10 0JP
Tel: 0191-423 6200
Fax: 0191-423 6201

Haipbiz

THE
SPONSORS
C·L·U·B

ISBN 0 9519585 1 8

Cover: Hidden 3
Back Cover: Group 2 *(Detail)*
Page 4: Situation 2 *(Detail)*
Page 54: Variations 1 *(Detail)*

Contents

PANAYIOTIS KALORKOTI

An

Exhibition

of

Acrylics

Watercolours

&

Etchings

Panayiotis Kalorkoti: Physiognomic Cartographies

Panayiotis Kalorkoti is an artist of extraordinary virtuosity. For all his versatility as a draughtsman, printmaker and painter, there has always been something in his approach of the jobbing professional, the master of his art and craft capable of brilliant and original response to the particularity of a commission, the challenge of a specific project. But to look back at his work in all its phases, from the inspired Art/Nature orderings of his Grizedale sequences, their keynote struck in the magisterial portrait of Bill Grant (the Grizedale Director) surrounded by the attributes of his vocation, to the mythicising documentation of his Gateshead National Garden Festival etchings and drawings, the evocative urban histories of the Hartlepool and Darlington collage-etchings and the stark combined inventories and iconographies of the Imperial War Museum Commissions, is to become aware of an informing graphic intelligence at the service of an inclusive humanism.

Kalorkoti is an artist committed to the truthful reflection of the conditions of modern life, aware of its complexities and uncertainties but determined that art is a means to the sharing of knowledge and understanding. The world can be imagined and pictured in art, realities discovered, ordered and represented. But underlying the plurality of modes and techniques of his practice, and unifying Kalorkoti's project as an artist, is his recognition of the ineluctable diversity of things: that there is no simple truth in representations of any kind; that there are as many realities as minds to imagine them; that there is no one history but many histories to any given political, social, cultural or personal situation; that 'communication' is capable of many forms, its contents of many configurations. Working often within the constraints of a public commission, or as an artist in residence, Kalorkoti has consistently carried this artistic project

7

into a conceptual space that is communal, performing the role of historian-memorialist, documenting and celebrating, concatenating events and objects into the simultaneities of the visual plane, and thereby re-configuring complex stories. It is an art that seeks an almost expository clarity; hence his predilection for series, sequences and grids, for repetition and variation of motif.

The configuring of two-dimensional elements of visual language on a flat surface to refer to things that exist, or might exist, in three-dimensional space and real time may be considered a kind of cartography. Lines, colours and tones, textures, and (in the case of collage) images borrowed from elsewhere, sometimes from quite other representational modes (as when a photographic image is incorporated into a multi-plate etching) are the components of an abstract mapping of certain aspects of reality: no map, however detailed, gets anywhere near to telling you the whole story of a place; no portrait tells you everything about a face. It's an awkward analogy, but one that I think would appeal to Kalorkoti in its suggestion that the various graphic media in which he chooses to work as an artist can provide truthful information about his subjects, and at the same time leave open the possibility of countless other representations: other maps for other journeys. As I have suggested, his is a democratic art, for time and again his imagery proposes access to a terrain of knowledge (natural, historical, cultural, personal) whose features are symbolically indicated to the willingly imaginative traveller.

The cartographical analogy may be taken further in connection with the works in this exhibition, in which Kalorkoti explores, with a characteristic serial rigour, the problems of portraiture. He has of course made many portraits in the past. The Gateshead commission of 1989-90, for example, included no fewer than 225 portrait drawings in a systematic record of the faces of people involved in the Festival, and a series of multi-plate etchings in which many of those faces appeared as the actors in the unfolding drama of the Festival's planning and realisation. As artist-in-residence at Leeds Playhouse in 1985 Kalorkoti was to observe in a number of paintings and etchings that the most intense emotions can be feigned, that artifice can convincingly create expression, that many characters can inhabit one face: it is not by chance that we speak of actors as 'portraying' their characters. There were ironies implicit in the 'playing of roles' that Kalorkoti was to exploit in numerous fictional 'Portraits' etched towards the end of the 1980s, and then, most movingly, in the 1989 'Soldier' series. These were shown at the Imperial War Museum in 1990, together with the two IWM commissioned prints, No. 1 of which features a frieze of photo-etched images of artists (Nash, Moore, Epstein, Spencer) juxtaposed with scenes of devastation, and No. 2 images of Chamberlain and Churchill in an ironic montage that remembers the contributions made by Spencer and Nash to the First War, and the high hopes that accompanied the institution of the Museum in 1920.

Kalorkoti has, then, thought long and deep about the representation of the human face and the nature of portraiture. In these recent works, made over the period of 1993-97, he has carried his investigations to new levels of intensity, concentrating, in a number of distinct series in various media, on the face alone, or in certain cases on group of faces. These unprecedented images are devoid of the social and political references which supply a situational or historical context to the portrayal of faces and figures in the earlier work. Imprecise in their figurings of physiognomic feature or shape of head the drama here is that of the representational process itself, the drama of a search for the image, of the emergence or disappearance of the subject. They do not aim at a likeness - whatever that may be! - so much as at an essential mapping of an unknown, and perhaps unknowable territory.

9

The research begins in earnest with the 'Unknown Head' series of 1993, whose strange and compelling peninsular and lagoon shapes might be those of rising smoke clouds, or of newly discovered coastlines, and whose textures suggest the evanescence of dappled light on water or the glare of hard sunlight on ancient rocks. These evocations of the aquatic and the mineral hint at the elemental, but the images maintain the human poignancy of Beckett's essential figures: in what ways are these heads 'unknown'? as unknown as the multitudes lost in war and holocaust? or as unknown as the nearest beloved? These heads simultaneously shadow into being and fade into nothingness. It is an effect achieved in other ways in the acrylic 'Studies for a Portrait' of 1994, in which several essays are made at what appears to be a single subject, but then again may not be; in the latest two (nos. 7 and 8) the face finally dissolves in the light/dark splash and dribble of the paint. The ambiguity in a project fated to remain forever as a series of 'studies', never to crystallize into the definitive portrayal, enacts the very problem it attempts to resolve and never will. Similar dissolutions of image into light and darkness, or translucency and opacity, as when a dot matrix photographic image is enlarged to the abstraction of black and white, occur in the double portraits of the 'Reflect', 'Situation' and 'Hidden' series of 1995, 1996 and 1997 respectively.

But what is the problem to be resolved? The portrait as genre comes loaded with cultural burdens: who shall be portrayed? why and how? What is the significance of 'likeness'? What does drawing, painting, etching do that photography doesn't or can't do? We are accustomed to the arguments that art can catch at the hidden 'character', that it goes beneath the surface, that it is charged with the 'insight' of the artist. But those are certainties we can no longer be sure of. Kalorkoti is keenly aware of the problematic status of the portrait in our time: by opting on the one hand for a linear graphic simplicity and the modest aims of documentary report, and on the other for a satirical comic-book starkness or direct photographic montage, he has succeeded in the highly effective portrayal of characters in situations that define some kind of meaning in the roles they play. He knows though that the representation of what is sometimes called psychological truth, the 'revelation of character' in a sitter, is no more than a fiction. The knowledge shared in these works is that some things cannot be known. It is not surprising, then, that recent portraits where figuration pretends to an accuracy of 'representation' the series should remain 'Untitled'. Even a likeness is no more than a rough mapping of terra incognita.

Mel Gooding

1.
Unknown Head 1 1993
Multi-Plate Etching
76.2 x 56.5cm (30 x 22$^{1}/_{4}$in) sheet
56.8 x 40.4cm (22$^{3}/_{8}$ x 15$^{7}/_{8}$in) imp.
Edition of 10

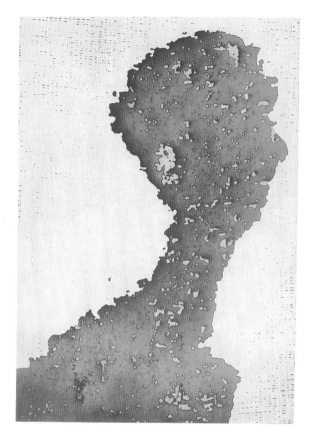

2.
Unknown Head 2 1993
Multi-Plate Etching
76.2 x 56.5cm (30 x 22$^{1}/_{4}$in) sheet
56.5 x 39.1cm (22$^{1}/_{4}$ x 15$^{5}/_{8}$in) imp.
Edition of 10

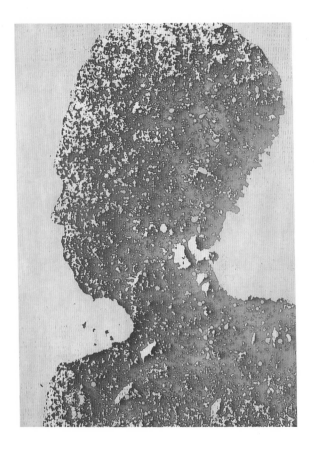

3.
Unknown Head 3 1993
Multi-Plate Etching
76.2 x 56.5cm (30 x 22^1/$_4$in) sheet
56.8 x 40cm (22^3/$_8$ x 15^3/$_4$in) imp.
Edition of 10

4.
Unknown Head 4 1993
Multi-Plate Etching
76.2 x 56.5cm (30 x 22^1/$_4$in) sheet
56.8 x 40cm (22^3/$_8$ x 15^3/$_4$in) imp.
Edition of 10

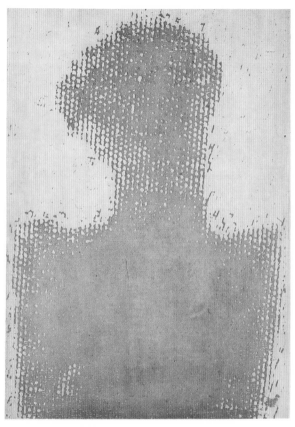

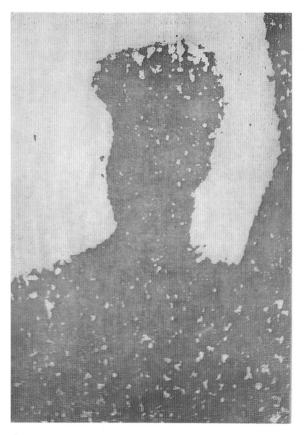

5.
Unknown Head 5 1993
Multi-Plate Etching
76.2 x 56.5cm (30 x 22^1/$_4$in) sheet
56.8 x 40cm (22^3/$_8$ x 15^3/$_4$in) imp.
Edition of 10

6.
Unknown Head 6 1993
Multi-Plate Etching
76.2 x 56.5cm (30 x 22^1/$_4$in) sheet
56.8 x 40cm (22^3/$_8$ x 15^3/$_4$in) imp.
Edition of 10

15

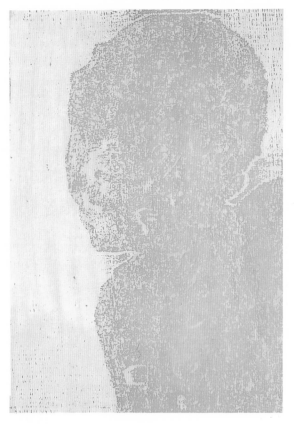

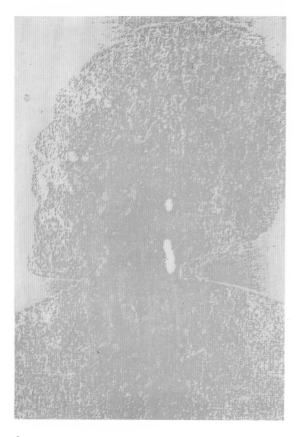

7.
Unknown Head 7 1993
Multi-Plate Etching
76.2 x 56.5cm (30 x 22^1/$_4$in) sheet
56.5 x 40cm (22^1/$_4$ x 15^3/$_4$in) imp.
Edition of 10

8.
Unknown Head 8 1993
Multi-Plate Etching
76.2 x 56.5cm (30 x 22^1/$_4$in) sheet
56.5 x 39.1cm (22^1/$_4$ x 15^3/$_8$in) imp.
Edition of 10

9.
**Study for a
Portrait 1** 1994
Acrylic on Paper
75.6 x 56.2cm
(29³/₄ x 22¹/₈in)

10.
**Study for a
Portrait 2** 1994
Acrylic on Paper
75.6 x 56.2cm
($29^3/_4$ x $22^1/_8$in)

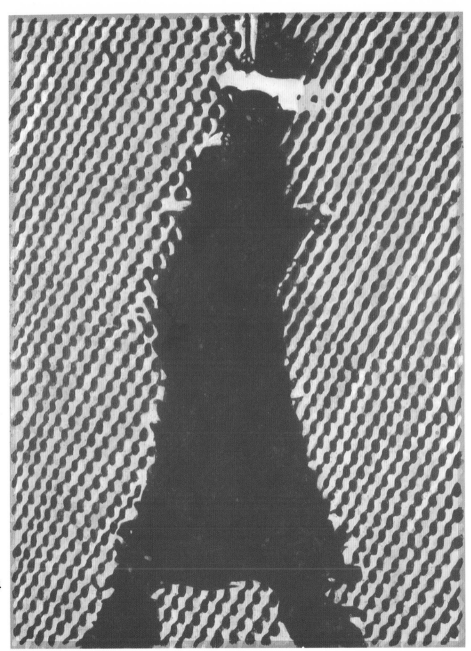

11.
**Study for a
Portrait 3** 1994
Acrylic on Paper
75.2 x 55.9cm
($29^5/_8$ x 22in)

12.
**Study for a
Portrait 4** 1994
Acrylic on Paper
74.9 x 55.9cm
(29^{1}/$_{2}$ x 22in)

13.
**Study for a
Portrait 5** 1994
Acrylic on Paper
75.2 x 55.9cm
(29$^5/_8$ x 22in)

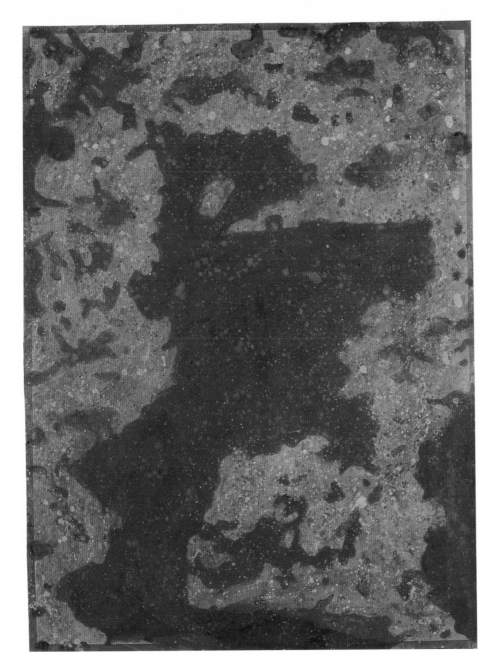

14.
**Study for a
Portrait 6** 1994
Acrylic on Paper
75.2 x 55.9cm
($29^{5}/_{8}$ x 22in)

15.
**Study for a
Portrait 7** 1994
Acrylic on Paper
75.6 x 56.2cm
(29^3/$_4$ x 22^1/$_8$in)

17. *DETAIL:*
**Study for a
Portrait 8**

16.
**Study for a
Portrait 8** 1994
Acrylic on Paper
75.6 x 56.2cm
(29³/₄ x 22¹/₈in)

18.
Untitled 1 1994
Watercolour
54.6 x 73.3cm
($21^{1}/_{2}$ x $28^{7}/_{8}$in)

19.
Untitled 2 1994
Watercolour
54.6 x 73.3cm
($21^{1}/_{2}$ x $28^{7}/_{8}$in)

20.
Untitled 3 1994
Watercolour
54.3 x 73.3cm
(21^3/$_8$ x 28^7/$_8$in)

21.
Untitled 4 1994
Watercolour
54.6 x 74cm
(21^1/$_2$ x 29^1/$_8$in)

27

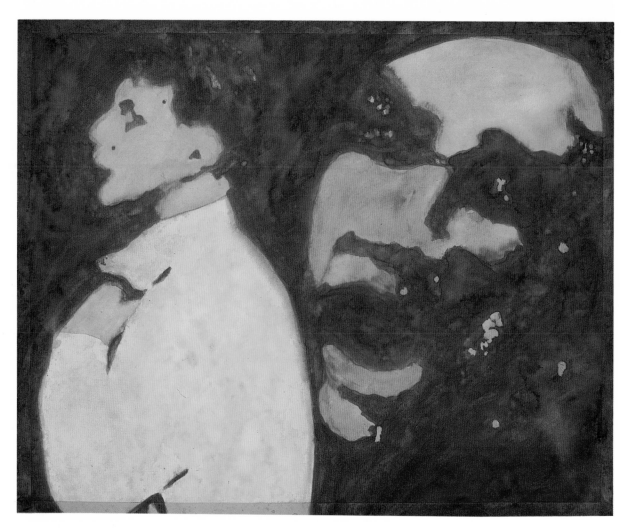

22. **Reflect 1** 1995
Watercolour
50.5 x 63.2cm (19^7/$_8$ x 24^7/$_8$in)

23. **Reflect 2** 1995
Watercolour
50.5 x 63.2cm (19$^7/_8$ x 24$^7/_8$in)

24. **Reflect 3** 1995
Watercolour
50.5 x 63.2cm (19^7/$_8$ x 24^7/$_8$in)

25. **Reflect 4** 1995
Watercolour
50.5 x 63.5cm (19$^7/_8$ x 25in)

26. **Group 1** 1996
    Acrylic on Paper
    51.1 x 72.4cm (20$^{1}/_{8}$ x 28$^{1}/_{2}$in)

27. **Group 2** 1996
   Acrylic on Paper
   51.1 x 72.4cm (20$^{1}/_{8}$ x 28$^{1}/_{2}$in)

28. **Situation 1** 1996
    Acrylic on Paper
    50.5 x 69.9cm (19$^7/_8$ x 27$^1/_2$in)

29. **Situation 2** 1996
Acrylic on Paper
50.5 x 69.9cm (19^{7}/$_{8}$ x 27^{1}/$_{2}$in)

30. **Watch** 1997
   Acrylic on Paper
   57.1 x 70.5cm (22$^{1}/_{2}$ x 27$^{3}/_{4}$in)

31. **Meeting** 1997
   Acrylic on Paper
   50.5 x 69.9cm (19$^{7}/_{8}$ x 27$^{1}/_{2}$in)

32.
Image 1 1996
Acrylic on Paper
76.2 x 57.1cm
(30 x 22^1/$_2$in)

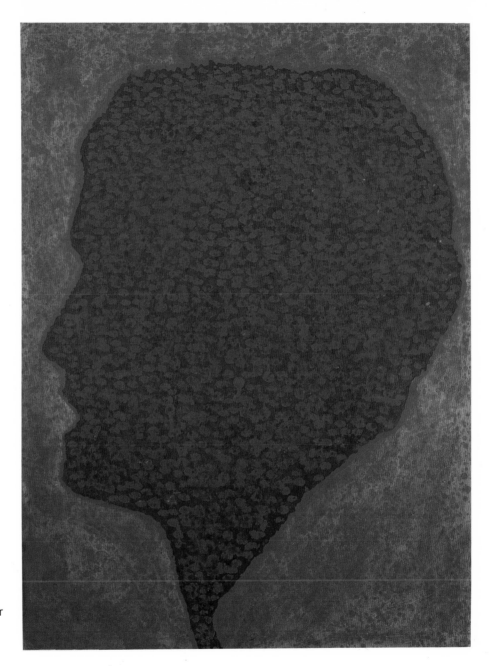

33.
Image 2 1996
Acrylic on Paper
76.2 x 57.1cm
(30 x 22¹/₂in)

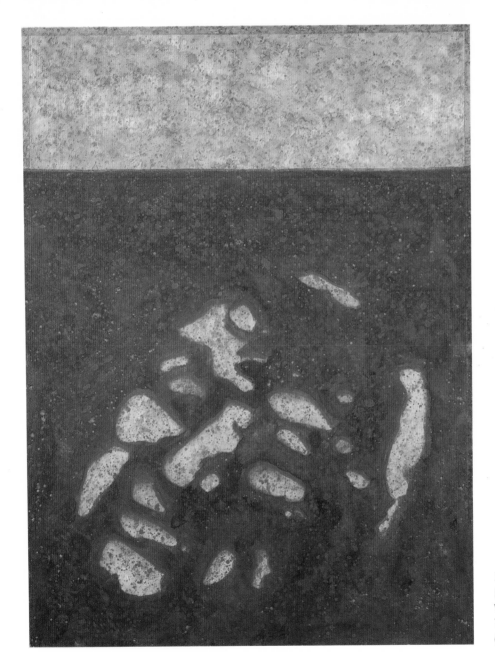

34.
Hidden 1 1997
Watercolour
76.5 x 57.5cm
($30^{1}/_{8}$ x $22^{5}/_{8}$in)

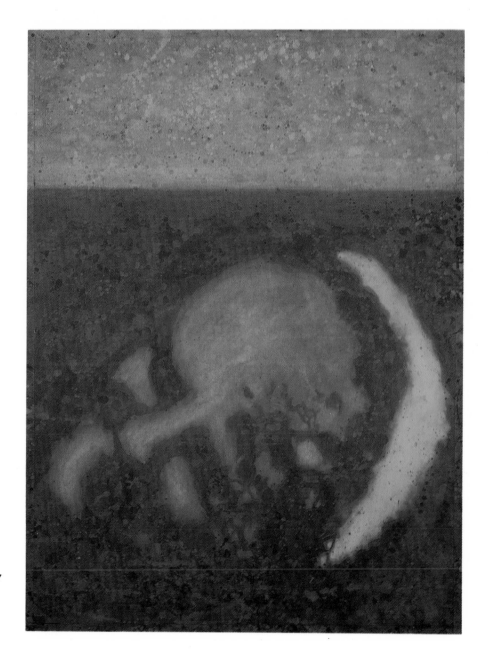

35.
Hidden 2 1997
Watercolour
76.5 x 57.5cm
($30^{1}/_{8}$ x $22^{5}/_{8}$in)

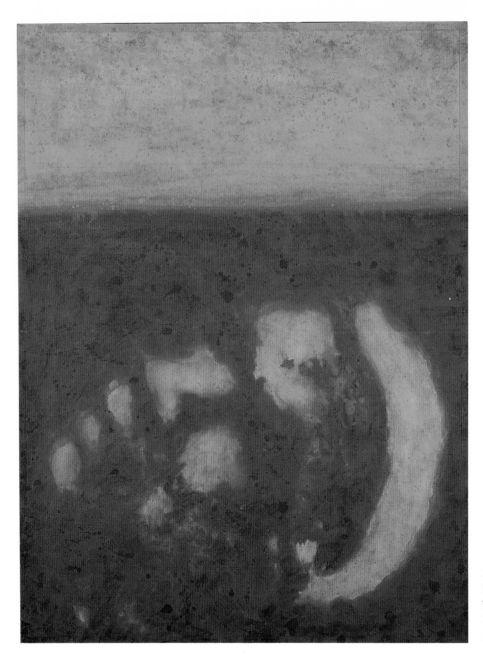

36.
Hidden 3 1997
Watercolour
76.5 x 57.5cm
(30$\frac{1}{8}$ x 22$\frac{5}{8}$in)

37.
Hidden 4 1997
Watercolour
76.5 x 57.5cm
($30^1/_8$ x $22^5/_8$in)

38. **Condition 1** 1997
 Acrylic on Paper
 50.5 x 69.9cm (19$^7/_8$ x 27$^1/_2$in)

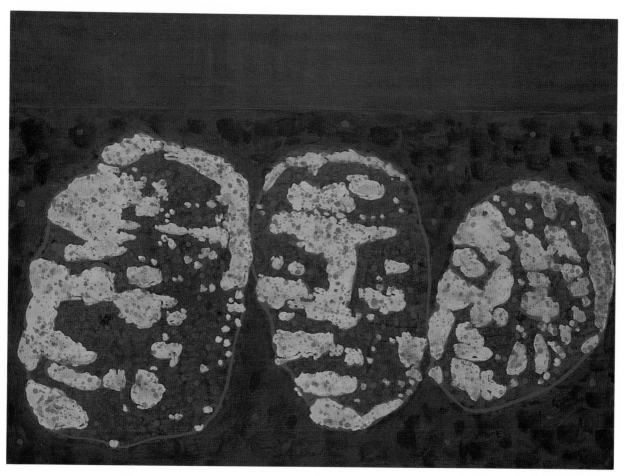

39. **Condition 2** 1997
Acrylic on Paper
50.5 x 69.9cm (19$^7/_8$ x 27$^1/_2$in)

40.
Passion 1 1997
Watercolour
76.5 x 57.5cm
(30^{1}/$_{8}$ x 22^{5}/$_{8}$in)

41.
Passion 2 1997
Watercolour
76.5 x 57.5cm
(30^{1}/$_{8}$ x 22^{5}/$_{8}$in)

42.
Movement 1 1997
Watercolour
74.9 x 55.9cm
(29$\frac{1}{2}$ x 22in)

43.
Movement 2 1997
Watercolour
74.9 x 55.6cm
(29$\frac{1}{2}$ x 21$\frac{7}{8}$in)

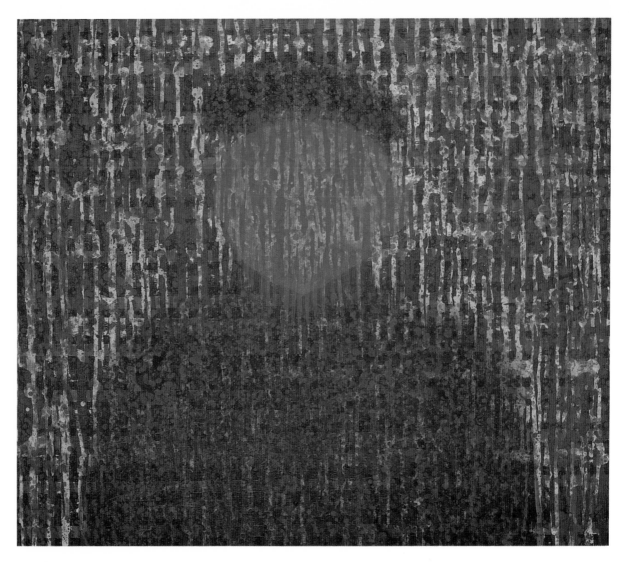

44. **One Figure** 1997
Acrylic on Paper
60.4 x 69.9cm (23³/₄ x 27¹/₂in)

45.
Into 1997
Acrylic on Paper
69.9 x 50.5cm
($27^1/_2$ x $19^7/_8$in)

Biography

1957   Born in Ayios Amvrossios, Cyprus

1976-80 Newcastle upon Tyne University, B.A. (Hons.) 1st Class in Fine Art

1982-85 Royal College of Art, London, M.A.

1985   Artist in Residence, Leeds Playhouse

1986-87 Koninklijke Akademie voor Kunst en Vormgeving, 's-Hertogenbosch
(Netherlands Government Scholarship)

1988   Bartlett Fellow in the Visual Arts (Newcastle upon Tyne University)
Commissioned by the Imperial War Museum, London; People's Theatre, Newcastle

1989   Commissioned by the Borough of Darlington; Borough of Hartlepool;
The Grizedale Society (also commissioned in 1991 and 1992)

1990   Commissioned by the National Garden Festival, Gateshead

1992   Artist in Residence, Cleveland

1994-95 Artist in Residence, The Grizedale Society

Taught part-time and visiting lecturer at a number of Art Colleges

Public Collections

Stedelijk Museum, Amsterdam
British Council, London
Imperial War Museum, London
Laing Art Gallery, Newcastle
University of Northumbria at Newcastle
Edinburgh University
Hatton Gallery, Newcastle University
Gray Art Gallery and Museum, Hartlepool
Darlington Arts Centre
Cleveland Gallery, Middlesbrough
Gallery in the Forest, Grizedale
Northern Arts
Rank Xerox
IBM

OVERLEAF
46. **Relief** 1996
Acrylic on Paper
60.7 x 57.1cm
(23$^{7}/_{8}$ x 22$^{1}/_{2}$in)

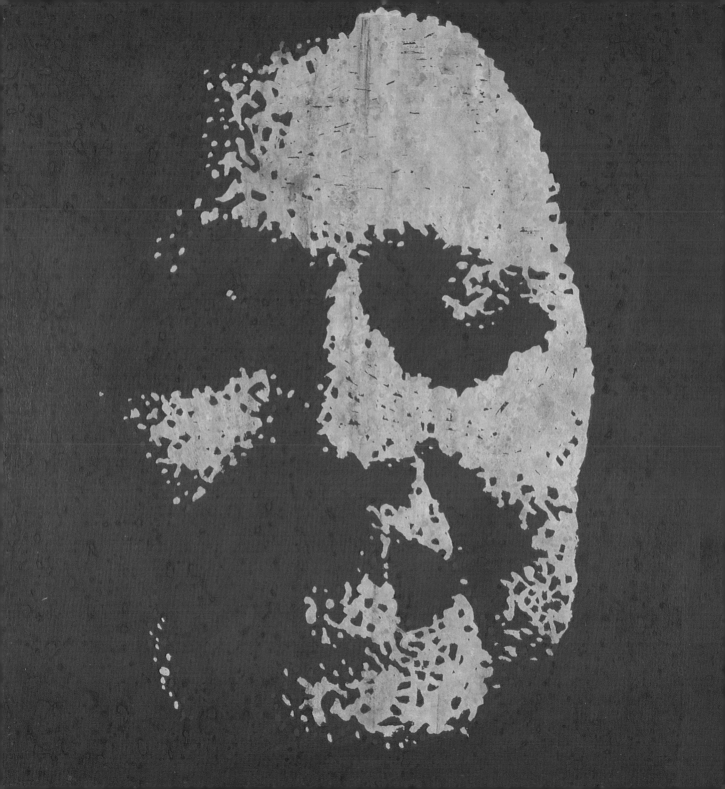

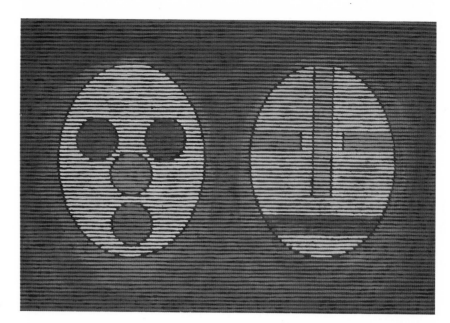

47.
Variations 1 1996
Acrylic on Paper
38.1 x 56.8cm (15 x 22³/₈in)

48.
Variations 2 1996
Acrylic on Paper
38.1 x 56.8cm (15 x 22³/₈in)

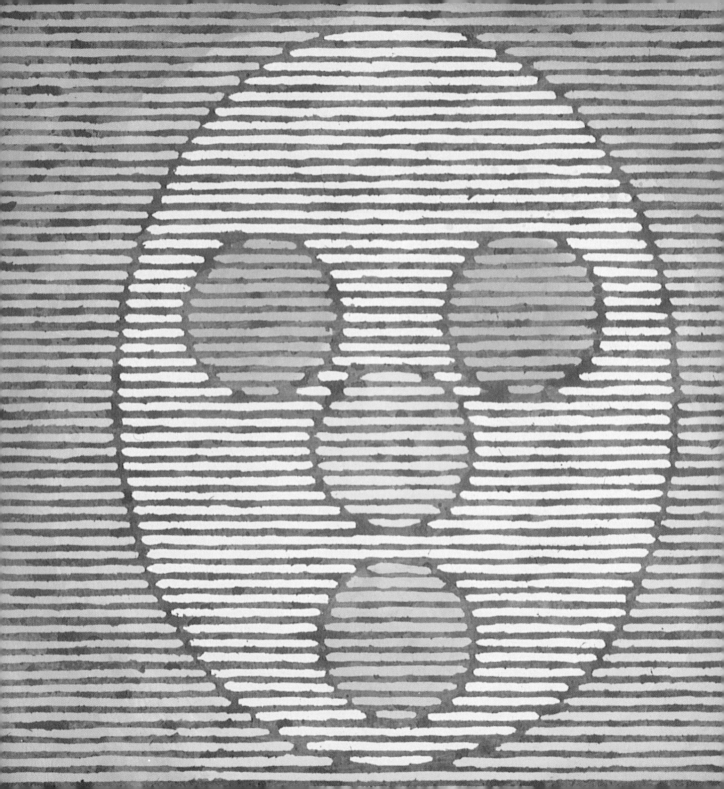

49.
Variations 3 1996
Acrylic on Paper
38.1 x 56.8cm (15 x 22³/₈in)

50.
Variations 4 1996
Acrylic on Paper
38.1 x 56.8cm (15 x 22³/₈in)

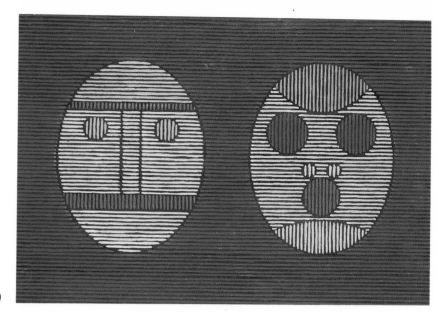

51.
Variations 5 1996
Acrylic on Paper
38.1 x 56.8cm (15 x 22³/₈in)

52.
Variations 6 1996
Acrylic on Paper
38.1 x 56.8cm (15 x 22³/₈in)

Selected Exhibitions

Solo Exhibitions

1980   Newcastle Polytechnic Gallery

1981   Bede Gallery, Jarrow
Hendersons Gallery, Edinburgh

1982   Bede Monastery Museum, Jarrow
Ceolfrith Gallery, Sunderland Arts Centre
Pentonville Gallery, London

1984   Abbot Hall Art Gallery and Museum, Kendal

1987   The Minories, Colchester
Steendrukkerij Amsterdam B.V.

1988-89   Hatton Gallery, Newcastle and tour: Darlington Arts Centre; Gray Art Gallery and Museum, Hartlepool; Queen's Hall Arts Centre, Hexham (Catalogue - text by Eva Krabbe)

1990   Imperial War Museum, London (Catalogue - text by Frank Whitford)
National Garden Festival, Gateshead (Catalogue - text by Roger Wollen)

1992   Design Works, Gateshead (Catalogue - text by Timothy Hyman)
Cleveland Gallery, Middlesbrough and tour: Steendrukkerij Amsterdam B.V. (Catalogue - text by Frank Van den Broeck)

1994   Gallery K, London and tour: Galerie Titanium, Athens (Catalogue - text by Roger Cardinal)

1995   Gallery in the Forest, Grizedale (Catalogue - text by Edward Lucie-Smith)

1997   Design Works, Gateshead (Catalogue - text by Mel Gooding)

Group Exhibitons

1980   The Stone Gallery, Newcastle

1981   *Small Works* Newcastle Polytechnic Gallery

1982   *and Printmaking* Waterloo Gallery, London (Catalogue)

1983   *Stowells Trophy* Royal Academy of Arts, London
Northern Young Contemporaries (awarded Granada Prize) Whitworth Art Gallery, Manchester

1984   Bath Festival Painting Competition
New Contemporaries ICA, London (Catalogue)

1985   *Printmakers at the Royal College of Art* Concourse Gallery, Barbican Centre, London (Catalogue - text by William Feaver)
Fresh Air St. Paul's Gallery, Leeds
Whitworth Young Contemporaries Whitworth Art Gallery, Manchester

1986   *Tradition and Innovation in Printmaking Today* Concourse Gallery, Barbican Centre, London and tour: Milton Keynes Exhibition Gallery; Ferens Art Gallery, Hull; Andrew Grant Gallery, Edinburgh; Aspex Gallery, Portsmouth (Catalogue)
Between Identity and Politics, A New Art Gimpel Fils, London and tour: Darlington Arts Centre; Gimpel and Weitzenhoffer, New York (Catalogue)
Fresh Art Concourse Gallery, Barbican Centre, London (Catalogue)
Whitechapel Open Whitechapel Art Gallery, London

1987   Athena Art Awards, Concourse Gallery, Barbican Centre, London
Which Side of the Fence Imperial War Museum, London

1989   *The Artistic Records Committee: A Retrospective 1972-1989* Imperial War Museum, London

1991   *Homage to Goya* and *Soldier* Museum of Modern Art, Oxford

1993   *The Portrait Now* National Portrait Gallery, London (Catalogue - text by Robin Gibson)
Gallery K, London (Catalogue - text by Mary Rose Beaumont)

1995   *Heads and Tales II* Herbert Art Gallery & Museum, Coventry

53.
Alone 1995
Acrylic on Paper
76.2 x 57.1cm
(30 x 22^1/$_2$in)